FIERCE FEMALES OF FICTION

PRINCESS LEIA

STAR WARS SENATOR TURNED HEROINE

Lorain Public Library System
351 W. Sixth St.
Lorain, OH 44052

KENNY ABDO

Fly!
An Imprint of Abdo Zoom
abdobooks.com

abdobooks.com

Published by Abdo Zoom, a division of ABDO, P.O. Box 398166, Minneapolis, Minnesota 55439. Copyright © 2021 by Abdo Consulting Group, Inc. International copyrights reserved in all countries. No part of this book may be reproduced in any form without written permission from the publisher. Fly!™ is a trademark and logo of Abdo Zoom.

Printed in the United States of America, North Mankato, Minnesota.
102020
012021

Photo Credits: Alamy, Everett Collection, Shutterstock
Production Contributors: Kenny Abdo, Jennie Forsberg, Grace Hansen
Design Contributors: Dorothy Toth, Neil Klinepier, Laura Graphenteen

Library of Congress Control Number: 2020910901

Publisher's Cataloging-in-Publication Data

Names: Abdo, Kenny, author.
Title: Princess Leia: Star Wars senator turned heroine / by Kenny Abdo
Other title: Star Wars senator turned heroine
Description: Minneapolis, Minnesota : Abdo Zoom, 2021 | Series: Fierce females of fiction | Includes online resources and index.
Identifiers: ISBN 9781098223144 (lib. bdg.) | ISBN 9781098223847 (ebook) | ISBN 9781098224196 (Read-to-Me ebook)
Subjects: LCSH: Organa, Leia (Fictitious character)--Juvenile literature. | Star Wars fiction--Juvenile literature. | Princesses--Juvenile literature. | Heroes--Juvenile literature. | Characters and characteristics in literature--Juvenile literature.
Classification: DDC 809.3--dc23

TABLE OF CONTENTS

Princess Leia 4

Backstory 8

Journey 14

Epic-Logue 20

Glossary 22

Online Resources 23

Index 24

PRINCESS LEIA

From royalty to powerful politician, Princess Leia will always be remembered as one of the Galaxy's greatest heroes.

Without the help of Leia, evil would have triumphed over good a long time ago.

BACKSTORY

Filmmaker George Lucas had an idea for an epic space **saga**. It would be a story about the battle between good and evil. The story would revolve around a troubled father at odds with his son and daughter.

Leia's character went through many **iterations**. Lucas first wrote her as a spoiled teenage royal princess. Then Leia was a civilian from a peaceful planet. At one point she was Luke Skywalker's cousin!

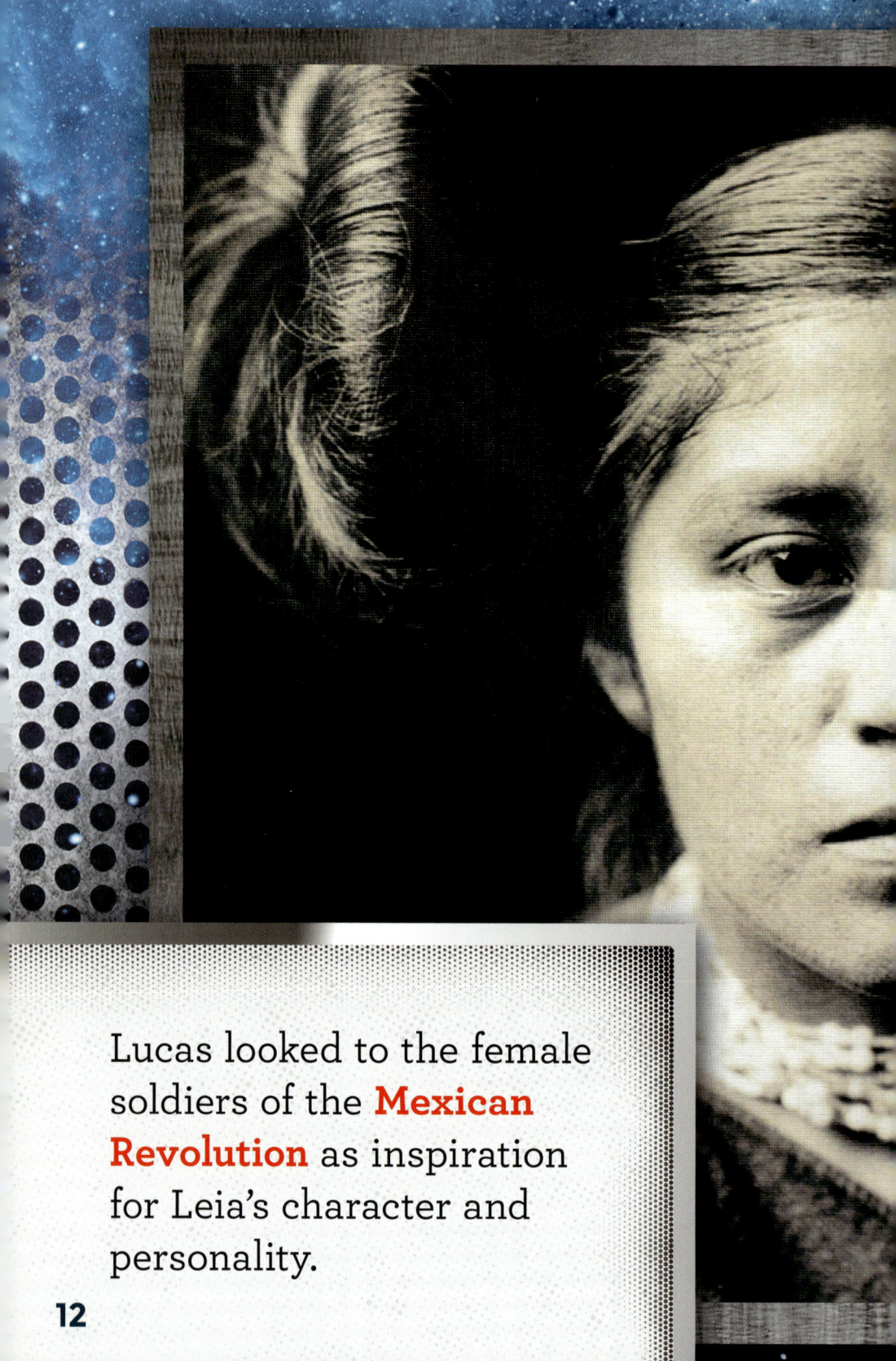

Lucas looked to the female soldiers of the **Mexican Revolution** as inspiration for Leia's character and personality.

Her iconic hair buns were inspired by females of the **Hopi** Native American tribe.

JOURNEY

Leia was born to Senator Padmé Amidala. She had a twin brother. They were separated and given to different families to keep them from their father who fell to the dark side.

Leia was raised as a Princess by **Viceroy** Organa of Alderaan. She eventually became senator of that planet. Alderaan was then blown up by the Death Star, and Leia was captured by Darth Vader.

Leia was rescued by Luke Skywalker, Han Solo, and Chewbacca. Together, they led a team to destroy the Death Star. Leia became a leader of the **Rebellion** against the Empire.

During the Battle of Endor, Leia learned that she and Luke were twins. And that Vader was their father. This meant that she too was force sensitive.

Leia became the leader of the Resistance of the First Order. She and Solo had a son named Ben. Leia dies while using the force to help save Ben, now Kylo Ren, from the dark side.

EPIC-LOGUE

Carrie Fisher beat more than two dozen actresses for the role of Leia. She was only 19 years old. Fisher's likeness as Leia has been portrayed in cartoons, video games, and books.

Princess Leia is seen today as a feminist **icon** and heroic role model for girls throughout planet Earth, not just in a galaxy far, far away.

GLOSSARY

Hopi – a Native American tribe known for its lifestyle of peace and goodwill.

icon – a person that is an object of great respect.

iteration – a new version of something.

Mexican Revolution – an uprising in Mexico to overthrow dictatorship that lasted from 1910 to 1920.

rebel – to rise against a ruler.

saga – a longform story of heroics and adventure.

Viceroy – a governor of an organized society in the name of a monarchy.

ONLINE RESOURCES

Booklinks
NONFICTION NETWORK
FREE! ONLINE NONFICTION RESOURCES

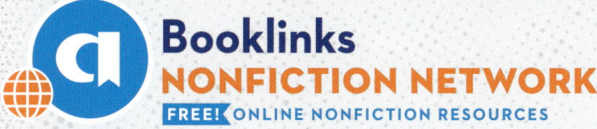

To learn more about Princess Leia, please visit **abdobooklinks.com** or scan this QR code. These links are routinely monitored and updated to provide the most current information available.

INDEX

Amidala, Padmé (character) 14

Chewbacca (character) 16

Darth Vader (character) 15, 17

Fisher, Carrie 20

inspiration 12, 13

Lucas, George 9, 11

media 20

Ren, Kylo (character) 18

Skywalker, Luke (character) 11, 16, 17

Solo, Han (character) 16, 18

Viceroy Organa (character) 15